moonflower
a Book of affirmations

edited by Irene Zahava

The Crossing Press, Freedom, CA 95019

Cover design by Rowan Silverberg

Printed in the U.S.A.

ISBN 0-89594-168-6

*Doorways are sacred to women for we
are the doorways of life and we must choose
what comes in and what goes out.*

—Marge Piercy

Everythin' we ever knew about the movement of the sea was preserved in the verses of a song. For thousands of years we went where we wanted and came home safe, because of the song.

—Anne Cameron

In every culture where the goddess is revered, women dance in ecstatic celebration of the sacred energy that can be felt and enjoyed in the body.

—Vicki Noble

i was cold/i was burnin up/a child
& endlessly weavin garments for the moon
wit my tears

i found god in myself
& i loved her/i loved her fiercely.
—Ntozake Shange

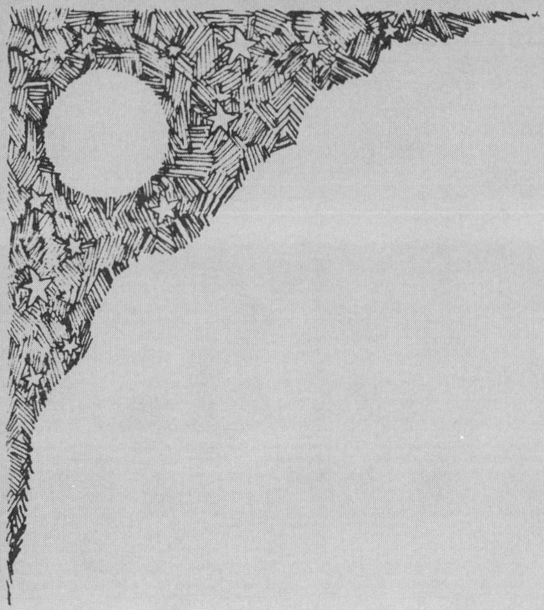

Love should grow up like a wild iris in the fields,
unexpected, after a terrible storm, opening a purple
mouth to the rain, with not a thought to the future . . .
—*Susan Griffin*

In the past all mountains moved in fire.
—*Yosano Akiko*

Let her
swim, climb mountain peaks, pilot airplanes,
battle against the elements, take risks,
go out for adventure, and
she will not
feel before the world ... timidity.
—*Simone de Beauvoir*

Let there be beauty and strength, power and compassion, honor and humility, mirth and reverence within you.
—Starhawk

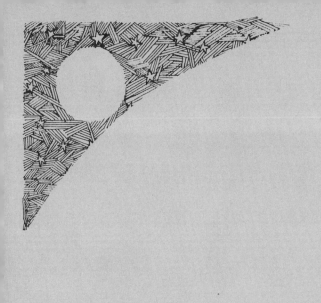

Broken and broken
again on the sea
The moon so easily mends.
—Chosu

When a woman loves a woman, it is the blood of the mothers speaking.
—Caribbean proverb

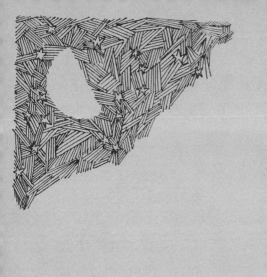

i am a warrior, a worker, a writer,
my grandmother's youngest daughter,
a feminist who does not believe in silence.
i am a woman who loves women,
i am a woman who loves myself.
—*Kitty Tsui*

as if the moon and you and I were slivers
of one mirror, gazing on herself at last.
—Robin Morgan

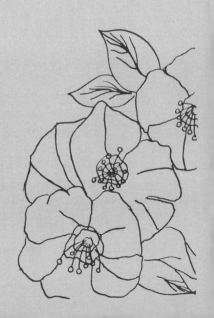

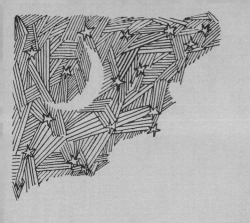

It is Crone-logically important to re-call that the word
friend *is derived from an Old English term meaning
to love, and that it is akin in its roots to an Old
English word meaning free. The radical friendship of
Hags means loving our own freedom, loving/en-
couraging the freedom of the other, the friend, and
therefore* loving fully.

—*Mary Daly*

Remember the plants, trees, animal life who all
  have their
tribes, their families, their histories, too. Talk
  to them,
Listen to them. They are alive poems.

—*Joy Harjo*

Every seed bursts its container.
—*Florida Scott-Maxwell*

This night the sun and moon dance . . .
—Marge Piercy

*The One Power that moves the Moon
Moves through you.*

—Marion Weinstein

*Freedom
is our real abundance.*
—Marge Piercy

*There was a time when you were not a slave,
remember that. You walked alone, full of laughter,
you bathed bare-bellied. You say you have lost all
recollection of it, remember . . . you say there are no
words to describe it, you say it does not exist. But
remember. Make an effort to remember. Or, failing
that, invent.*

—Monique Witting

*One of the cardinal rules for the practice of magic
or psychic work of any kind is to make a protective
circle around oneself for grounding. Then the soul
can fly like an eagle, while the body remains
nourished and protected within the magical space.*

—Vicki Noble

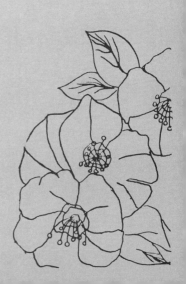

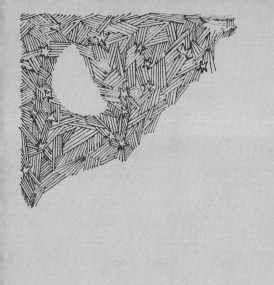

Remember the sky that you were born under,
know each of the star's stories.
Remember the moon, know who she is.

—Joy Harjo

You are a witch by being female, untamed, angry, joyous and immortal.

—*Source unknown*

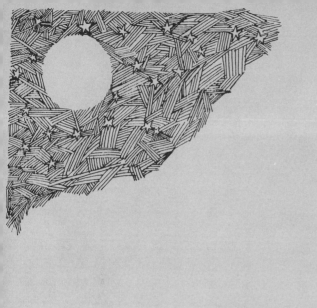

It took me more than twenty years, nearly twenty-five, I reckon, in the evenings after supper when the children were all put to bed. My whole life is in that quilt. . . . my hopes and fears, my joys and sorrows, my loves and hates. I tremble sometimes when I remember what that quilt knows about me.

—Marguerite Ickis, quoting her great-grandmother

Sleeping, turning in turn like planets
rotating in their midnight meadow:
a touch is enough to let us know
we're not alone in the universe, even in sleep . . .
—Adrienne Rich

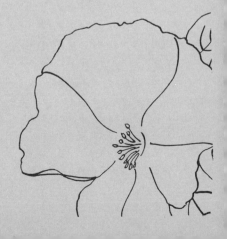

I send you water from the moon—
impossible to hold.
—*Javanese saying*

*With a certain amount of concentration, a person
doing yoga may begin hearing a gentle humming
that recalls the sound of dragonfly wings.*
—Vicki Noble

When a great adventure is offered,
you don't refuse it.
—*Amelia Earhart*

We are the flow, we are the ebb,
We are the weavers, we are the web.
—Shekinah Mountainwater

The most important thing one woman can do for another is to illuminate and expand her sense of actual possibilities . . .
—Adrienne Rich

*Music has to be played with love and, where it is,
it brings people together.*
—Mary Lou Williams

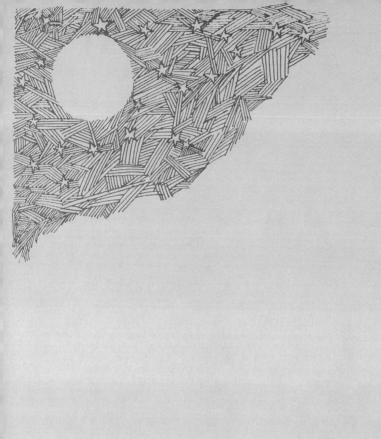

*I'll wrap four strands of hair
around a notch of the nearest pine.*

A spider's web, come Spring.
—Roberta Hill Whiteman

Listen. We are making ready. Hear our music across the dying land.
—*Martha Courtot*

The last treasures we have, the secrets of the matriarchy, can be shared and honoured by women, and be proof there is another way, a better way, and some of us remember it.

—Anne Cameron

She Who floods like a river and
like a river continues
She Who continues
—*Judy Grahn*

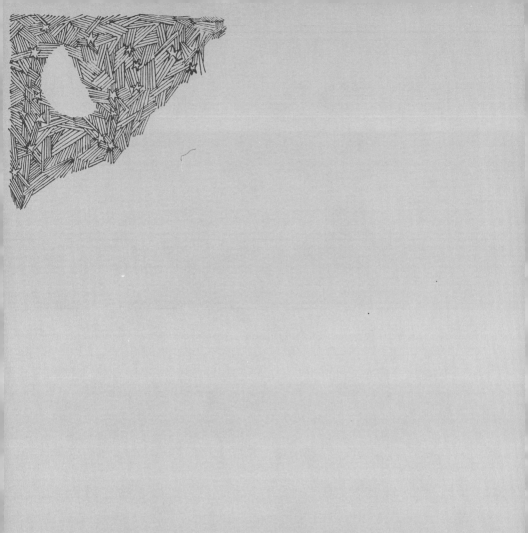

may I never forget
the warning of my woman's flesh
weeping at the new moon
—*Audre Lorde*

*Change of life by definition refers to the future;
one life is finishing therefore another life must be
beginning. . . . There is no more beautiful word in
the language than withered.*
—June Arnold

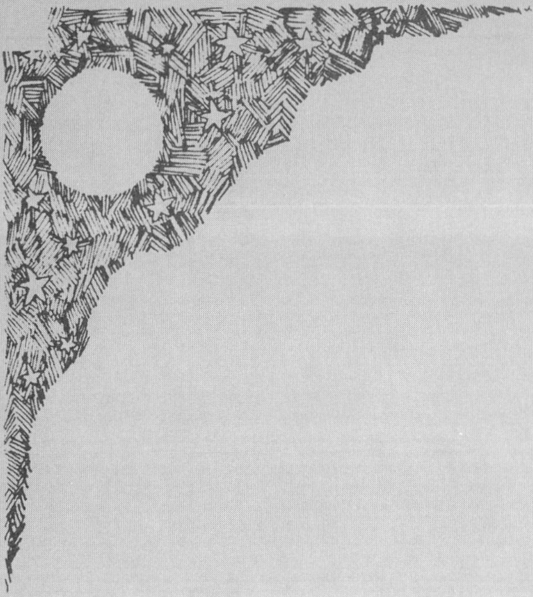

All trees are sacredly possessed by an unseen life, but above all fruit trees are sacred. Earth sends up fruits, with the help of the moon.
—Anne Kent Rush

At one time it was believed that the moon was a hive from which all honey came.

—Source Unknown

We seek not rest but transformation.
We are dancing through each other as doorways.
—*Marge Piercy*

She changes everything she touches,
And everything she touches, changes.
—Starhawk

A woman has to know patience, and a woman has to know how to stick it out, and a woman has to know all kinds of things that don't just come to you like a gift.

—Anne Cameron

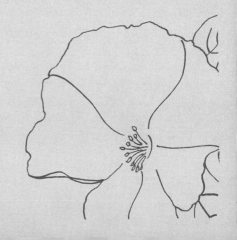

*I took a deep breath and listened to the old bray of
    my heart.
I am, I am, I am.*
—Sylvia Plath

*It is said that Eskimo women who are close friends
have a way of singing together in which, placing
their open mouths together, they alternately "play"
each others' vocal chords by sympathetic vibration to
their own song.*

—Lee Lanning and Nett Hart

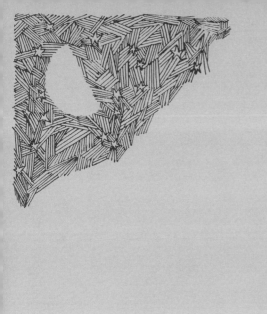

I have noticed that as soon as you have soldiers the story is called history. Before their arrival it is called myth, folktale, legend, fairy tale, oral poetry, ethnography. After the soldiers arrive, it is called history.
—Paula Gunn Allen

What would happen if one woman told the truth
  about her life?
The world would split open
—*Muriel Rukeyser*

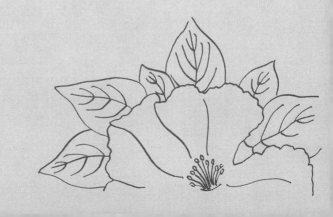

The erotic is a resource within each of us that lies in a deeply female and spiritual plane, firmly rooted in the power of our unexpressed or unrecognized feeling.
—Audre Lorde

The original power of the female group to harness and use fire is acknowledged in mythology all over the world and pertains to the sexual fire as well as the use of physical fire for cooking and transformation mysteries.

—Vicki Noble

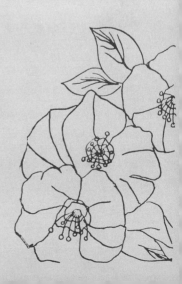

In ancient times moon-priestesses were called "virgins," meaning "not married, not belonging to a man, a woman who was One-in-Herself." The word derived from a root meaning "force, strength."
—Monica Sjoo and Barbara Mor

*In this circle I pass each of you a shell from our
    mother sea
Hold it in your spirit and hear the stories she
    will tell you*
—Crystos

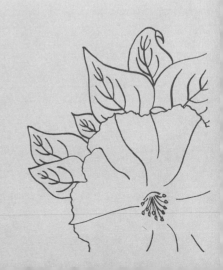

The earth, the water, the fire, the air
Returns, returns, returns, returns.
—Native American chant

The women begin talking among themselves.
They are together to perform a ceremony.
Rituals of women take time.
There is no hurry; time stands still.

—Beth Brant

My time is carved in my poems
like the years of a tree in its rings
like the years of my life in my wrinkles.
—Leah Goldberg

Remember that you are this universe and that this universe is you.
Remember that all is in motion, is growing, is you.
—Joy Harjo

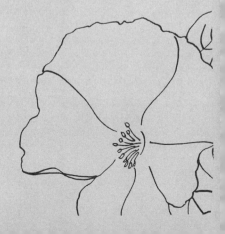

I cannot live without my life!
—Emily Bronte

I have made friends with the night.
—Jane Byrd

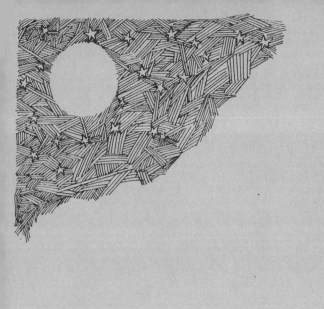

There are Women everywhere with fragments
gather fragments
weave and mend
When we learn to come together we are whole

—Anne Cameron

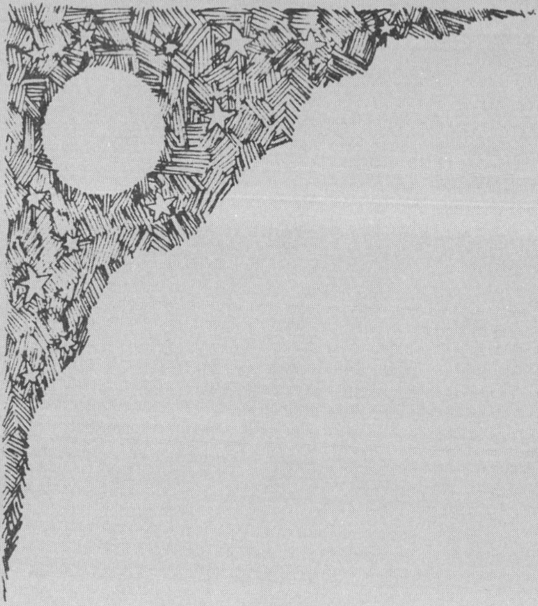